39 Animals Mandala in this book

THIS BOOK BELONGS TO

_____

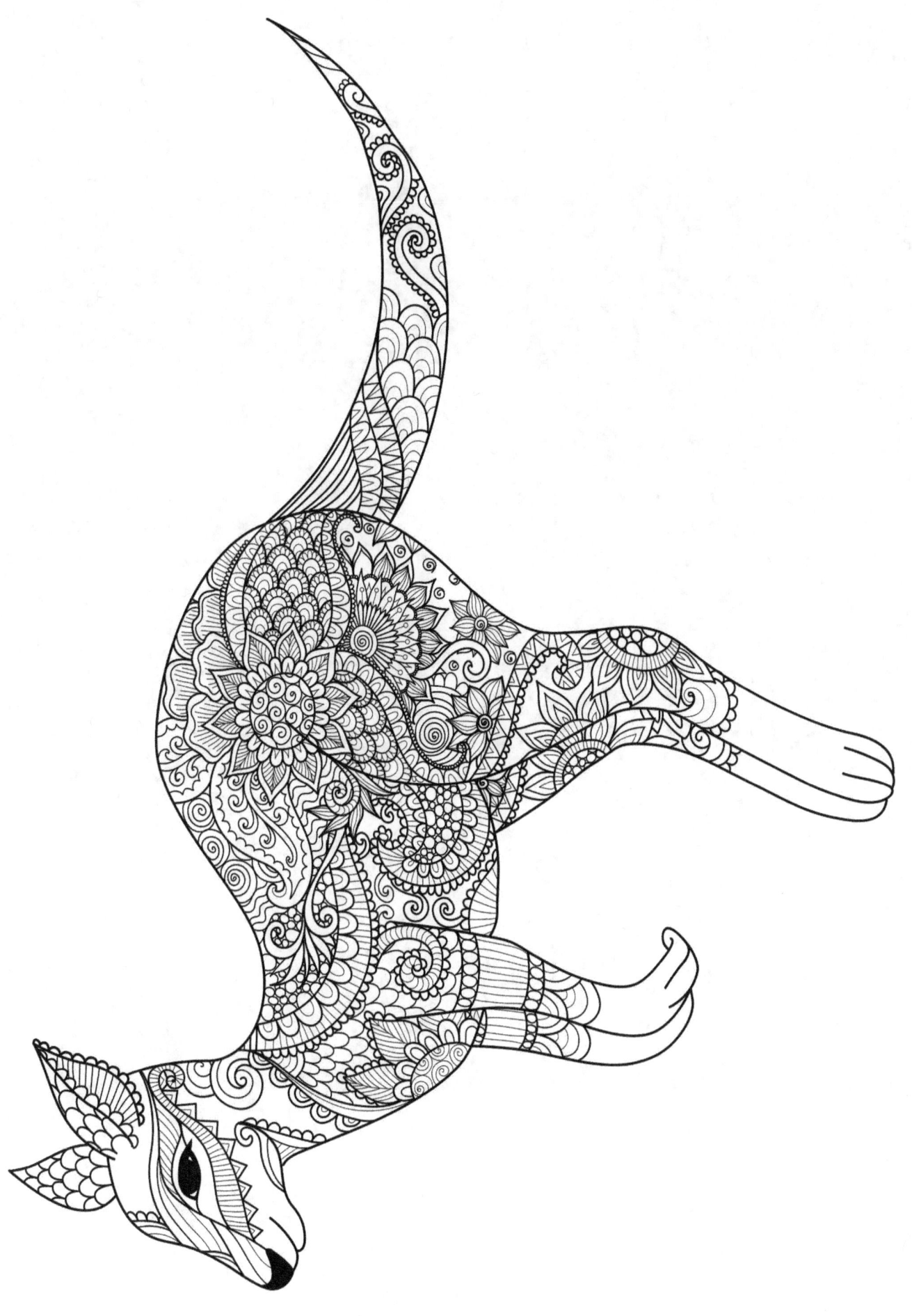

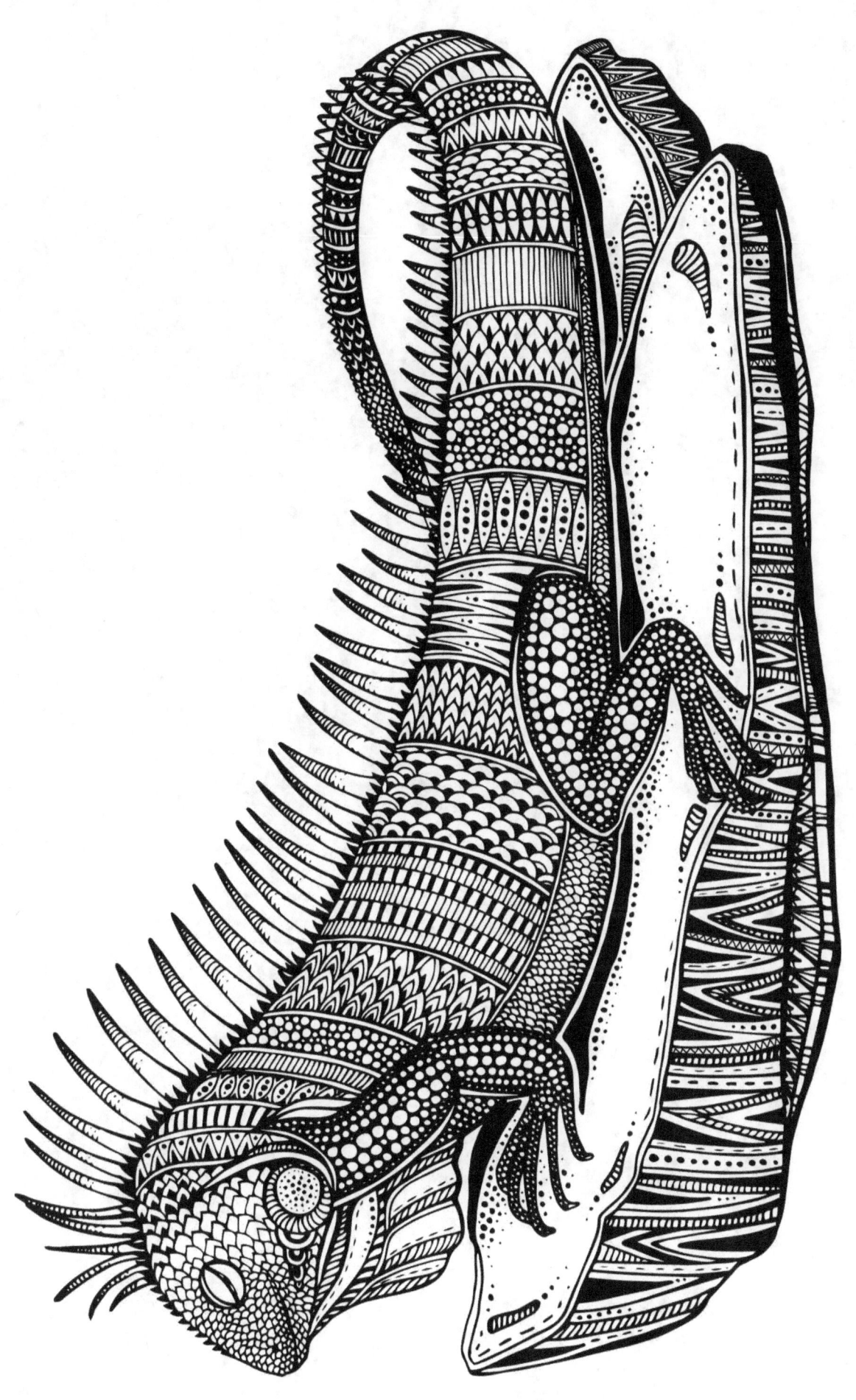

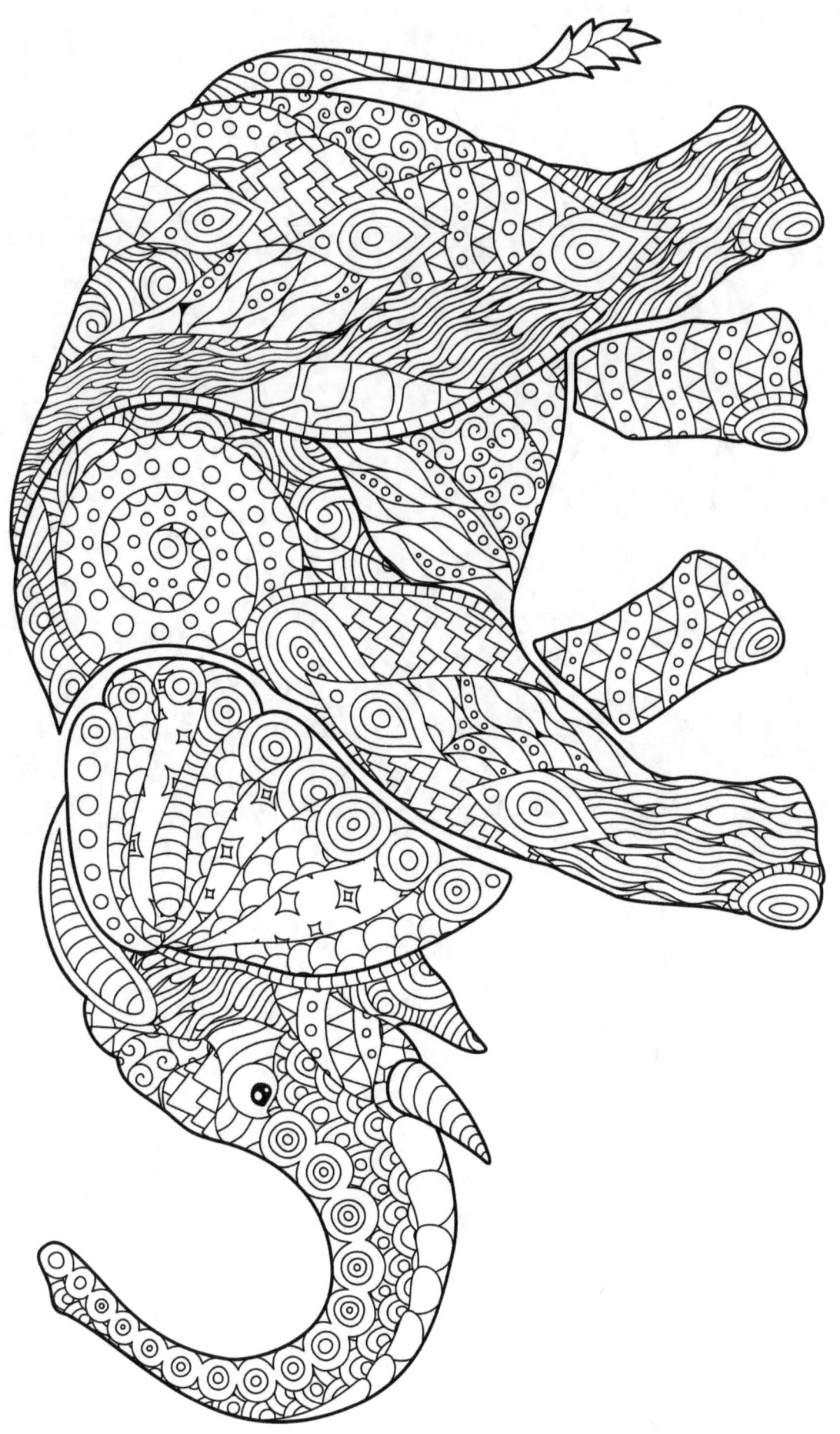

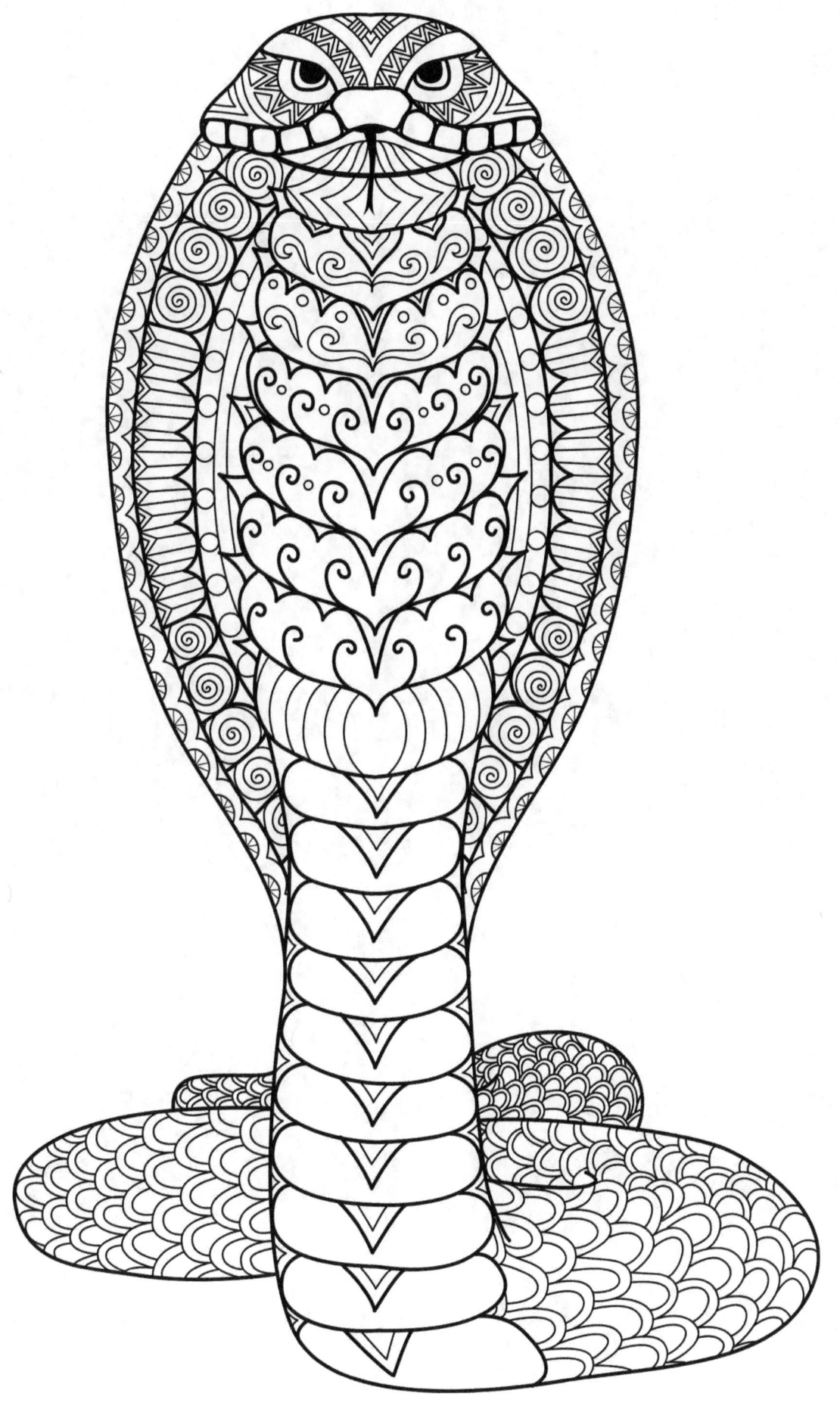

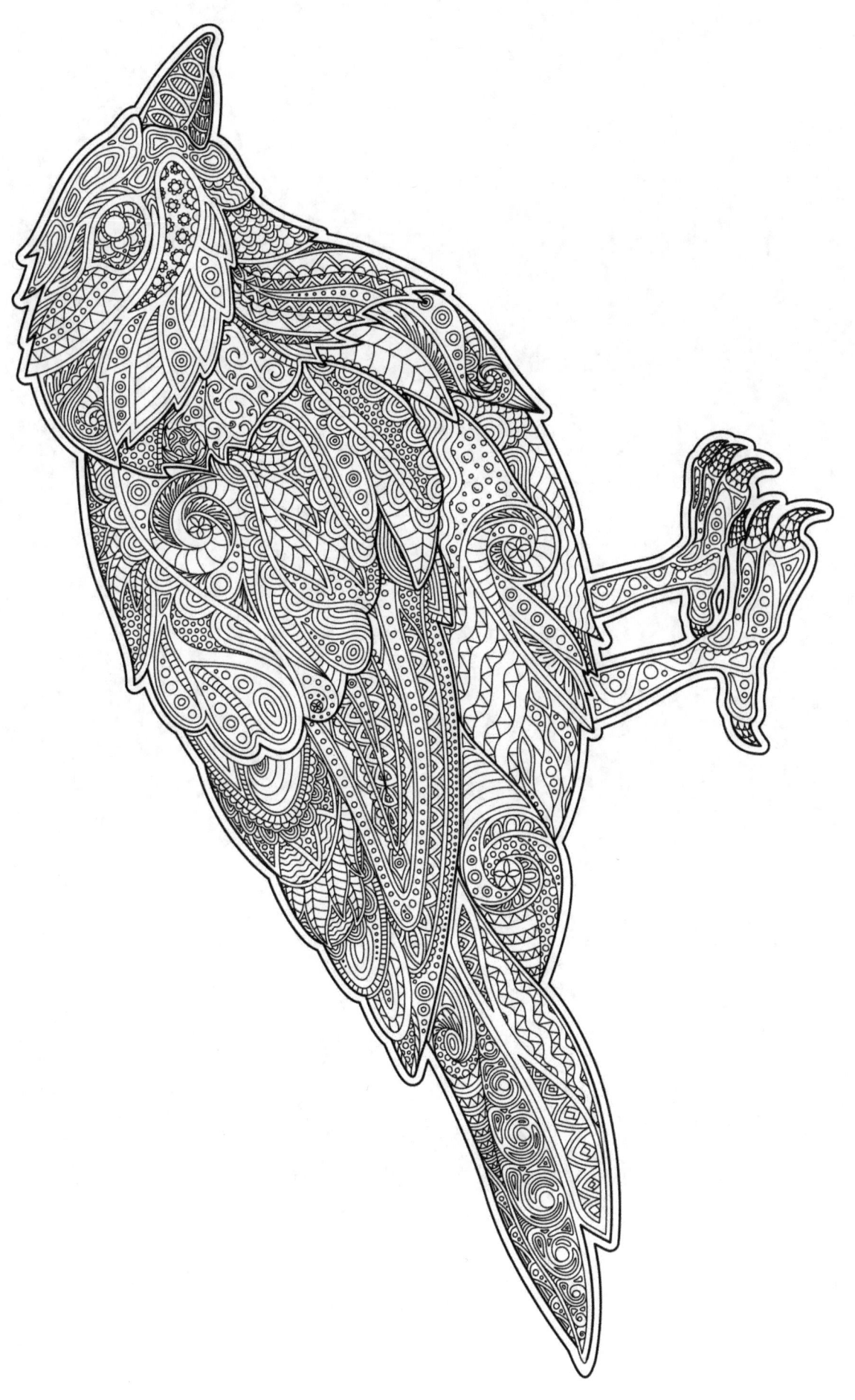

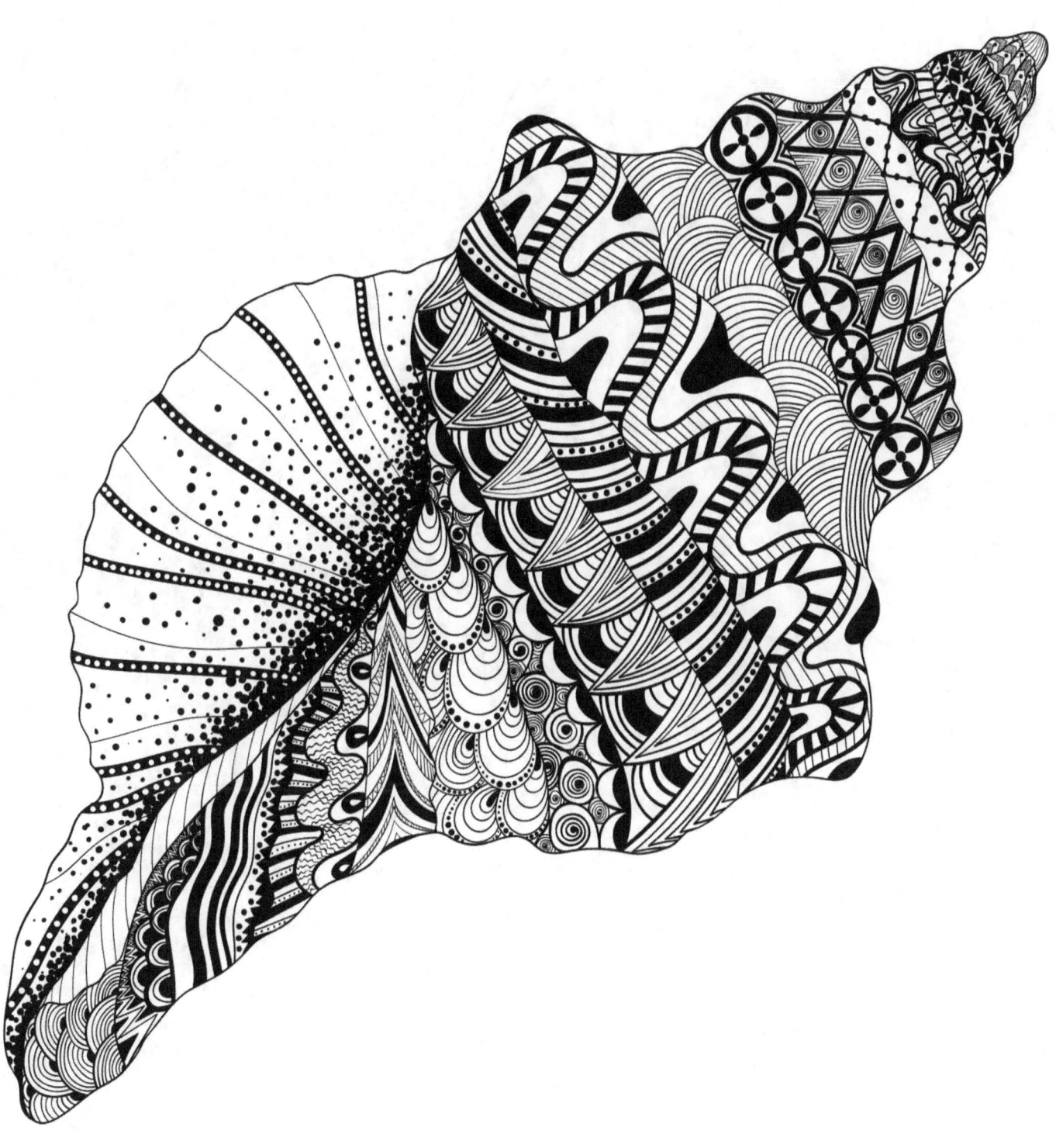

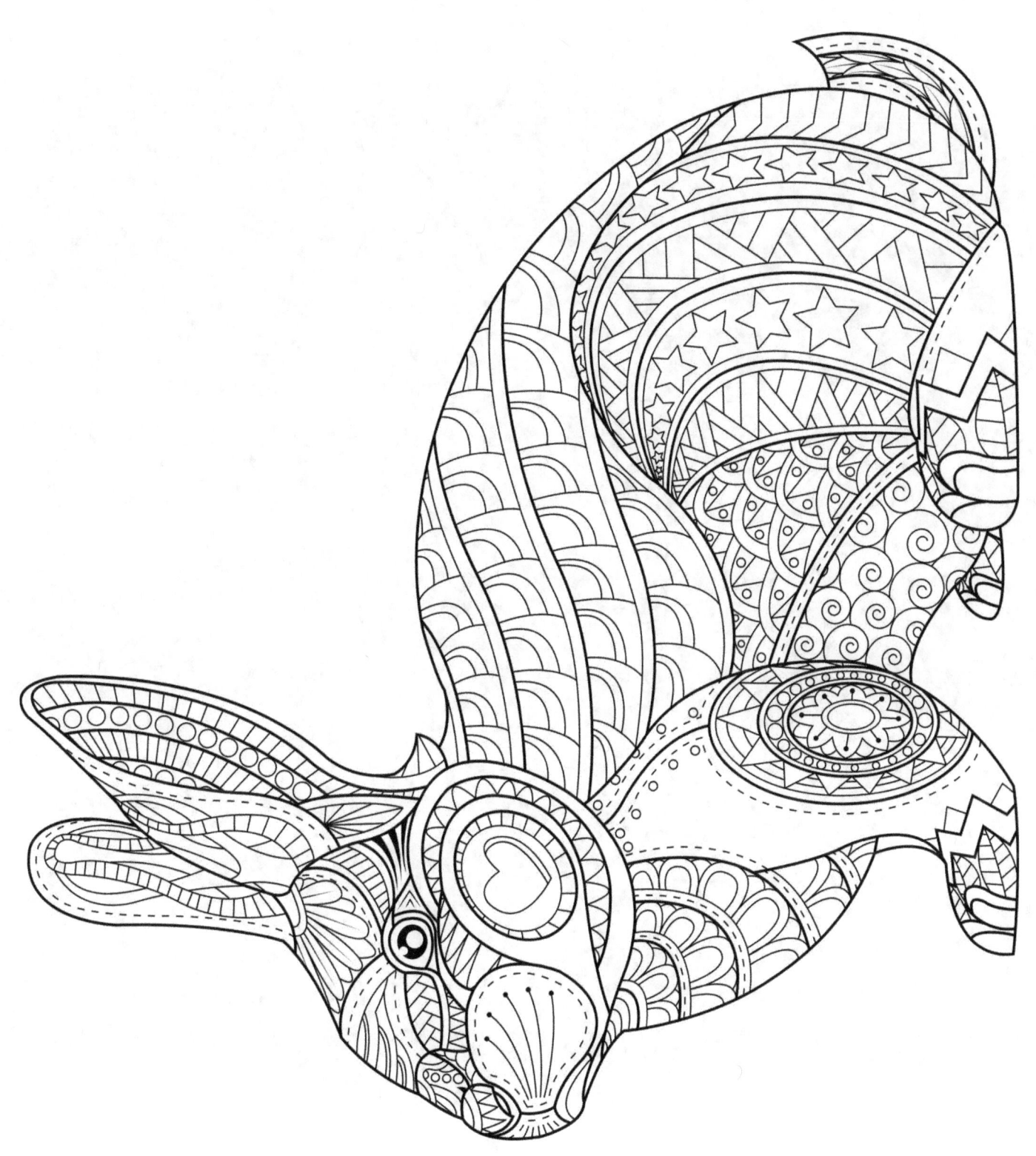

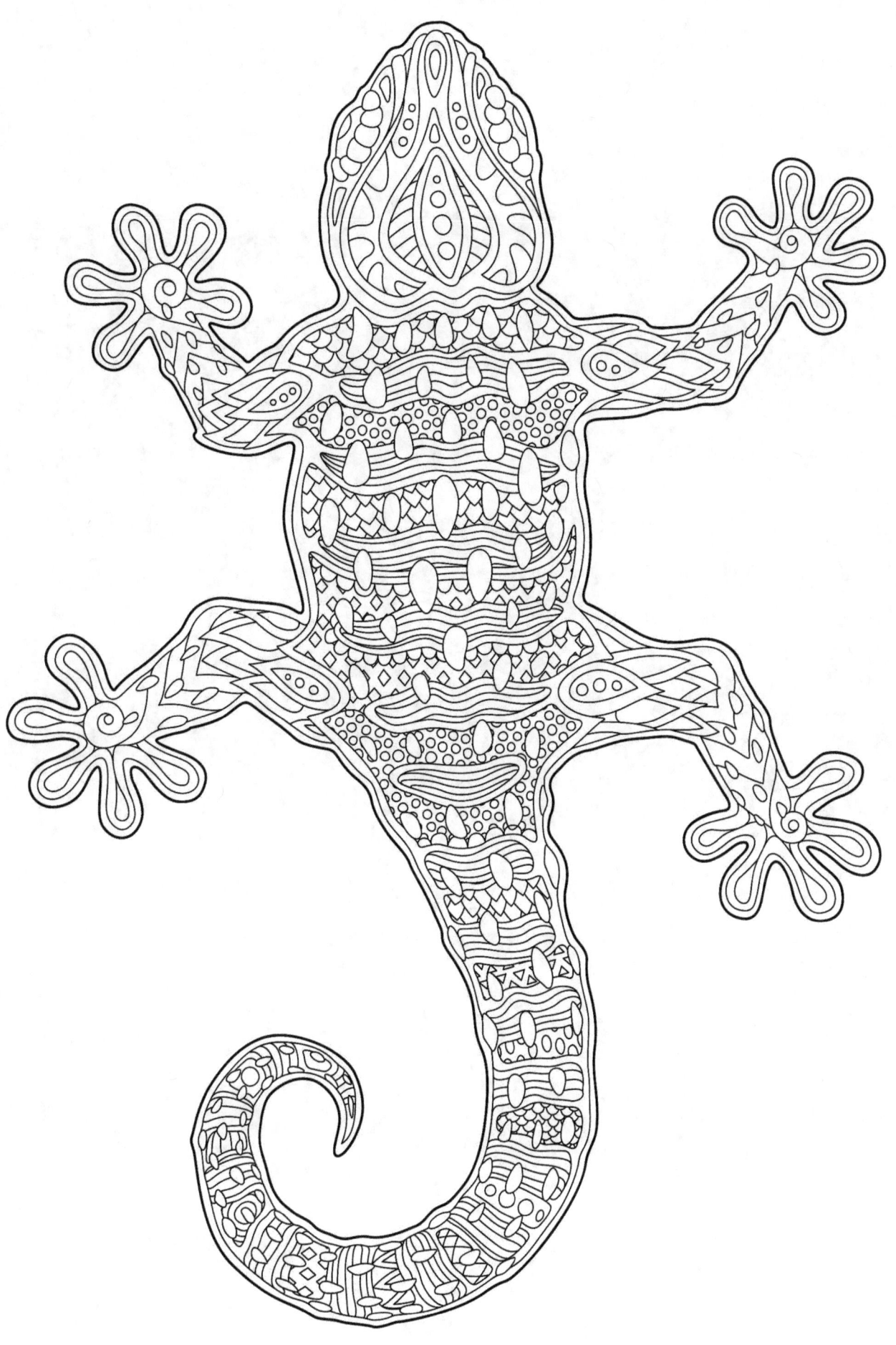

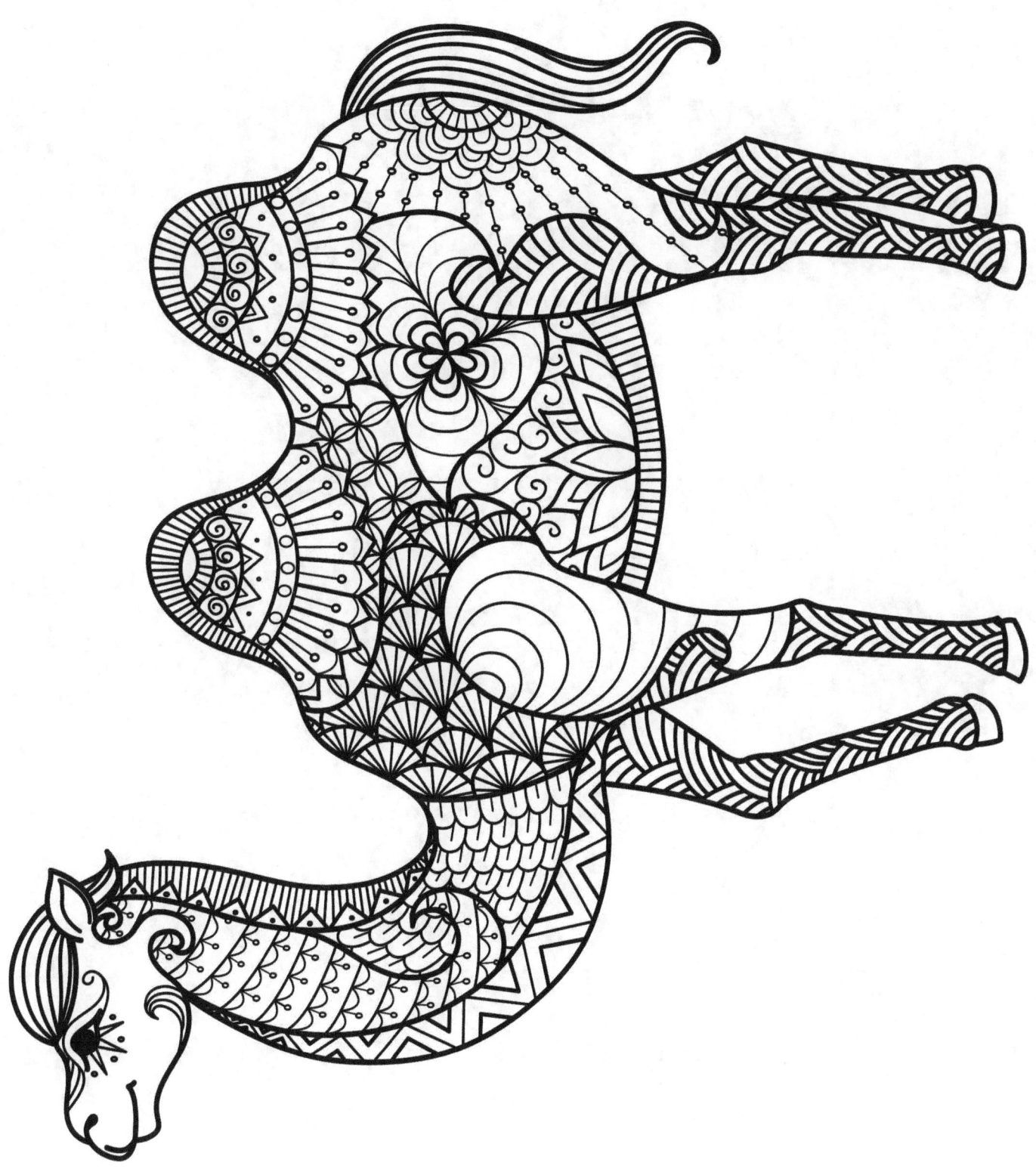

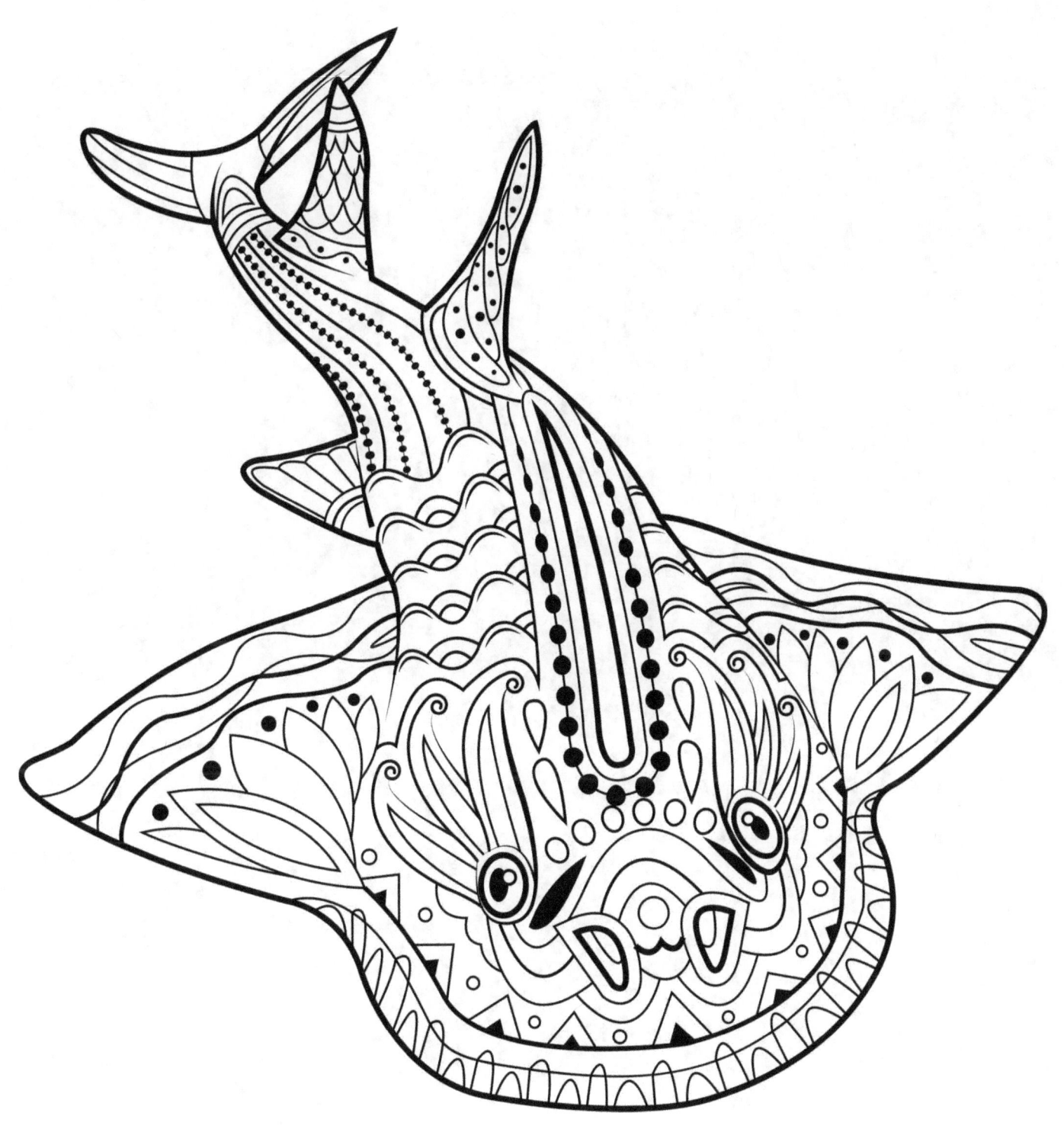

Example From Adult Coloring Book **Vol.5**

Animal Head Mandala Patterns

THANK YOU

www.ingramcontent.com/pod-product-compliance
Lightning Source LLC
Chambersburg PA
CBHW081409280526

45788CB00009B/3033